Fixed Layout ePub
A Practical Guide to Publish eBooks from PDF Files

Éric Dodémont

CreateSpace
2014

- The eBook version of this book is a fixed layout ePub document. The layout has been made with the *Scribus* software, and the conversion from PDF to ePub has been made by following the method described in this book (using *pdf2htmlEX*).

- In this book, we are using mainly the *Linux* operating system, but everything should also be possible with *Microsoft Windows* (PC) or *Apple OS X* (Mac).

- The following versions are used in this book: *pdf2htmlEX* version 0.11 and 0.12, ePub specifications 3.0 and 3.0.1.

About the author: Engineer in a Telecom company. Master degree in electronics engineering.

Title of the first edition: *A Practical Guide to Convert a PDF File to an ePub Version 3 Fixed Layout File: With Free Open Source Tools*.

© Éric Dodémont, Liège, Belgium.
Second edition: November 2014. ISBN: 978-1502809506.
First edition: May 2014.
www.dodeeric.be — info@dodeeric.be

Fixed Layout

Different file formats exist for fixed layout eBooks. Bellow a list of the main ones:

- PDF (Portable Document Format) [.pdf]
- ePub (electronic Publication) [.epub]
- Apple iBooks (similar to ePub) [.ibooks]
- Amazon Kindle (similar to ePub) [.kf8]
- DjVu (Déja Vu) [.djvu]

Fixed layout eBooks can be bought on different online stores. Bellow a list of some of them:

- Google Play Books (ePub & PDF)
- Apple iBooks (ePub & iBooks)
- Kobo (ePub)
- Amazon (KF8)

In this book, we will focus on the conversion of a PDF file to a fixed layout ePub file. This is possible since the version 3 of the ePub format specifications which includes now the fixed layout mode in addition to the traditional flowing text mode.

This type of conversion can be very useful as the page layout / desktop publishing (DTP) softwares are always exporting the final result as a PDF file (optimized for paper or online publication).

The ePub 3 fixed layout (FXL) format specifications published by the *International Digital Publishing Forum* (IDPF) can be found here:

www.idpf.org/epub/fxl

The latest ePub version 3.0.1 specifications for fixed layout can be found here:

www.idpf.org/epub3/latest/publications#sec-package-metadata-fxl
www.idpf.org/epub3/latest/contentdocs#sec-fixed-layouts

A Field Guide to Fixed Layout for E-Books published by the *Book Industry Study Group* (BISG) is available for free here:

www.bisg.org/publications/field-guide-fixed-layout-e-books

The ePub version 3 publication format uses all the modern Web technologies like HTML5, CSS, JS, SVG, WOFF, XML, XHTML, etc. Be aware that there are sometimes some restrictions when these technologies are used for ePub documents. For example, in ePub version 3, only the SVG version 1.1 can be used, not the version 1.2 (not yet released, but already in use); the `direction` and `unicode-bidi` properties must not be included in stylesheets, etc.

Important remarks:

1) This book is only about fixed layout ePub. Fixed layout can be used if the book has a sophisticated layout with lots of images. Such fixed layout books are usually made with desktop publishing programs like *Scribus*, *Adobe InDesign*, *Quark XPress*, or *Microsoft Publisher*. For books with only text and with no or few images, a flowing text ePub is more suitable and more easy to do.

2) Most of the PDF to ePub converters do not work for sophisticated layout because they convert a fixed layout PDF into a flowing text ePub, which gives most of the time an ugly and unusable result unless the file is heavily adapted. They just extract the text and the images from the PDF, and put then sequentially into a flowing text ePub with all the layout gone.

3) Most of the ePub reader/viewer applications do not support (yet) the fixed layout. If you try to display a fixed layout ePub with such readers, the result will be ugly and unusable. Good ePub readers supporting the fixed layout are:

• For *Android* and *iPad* tablets: *Gitden*, *Google Play Books*.
• For *Windows* and *Mac* computers: *Readium* (also for *Linux*; it is a *Google Chrome browser extension), Adobe Digital Edition (latest version 4.0)*.

Most of the time, small screens are not suitable for fixed layout eBooks, because it can happen you will have to zoom and pan into the content. Such eBooks should be preferably read on tablets rather than on smartphones.

4) Even if in this book we are only talking of producing a fixed layout ePub document from a PDF document (which has always a fixed layout), there is another method to produce such ePub, which can be called "native": saving the final result directly in the ePub-fxl format from the DTP program, without using an intermediate format like PDF. As from now, only *InDesign CC* (2014) can do that. Of course, a lot of books are available since years only in PDF format, making the method explained hereafter very useful.

Conversion Methods

There are three main methods to convert a PDF file to a fixed layout ePub file:

1) Method 1: Bitmap image only + Hidden text

Each ePub page is a bitmap image (PNG8, possibly PNG24 or JPEG) of an exact replica of the PDF page. This bitmap image is the result of the rendering of the text (using vector fonts), bitmap images, and vector images. To maintain accessibility (select text, copy/paste text, search text, indexing text, text to speech, etc.), an invisible text layer is added on top of the image. This is also the way used to convert a PDF file to a DjVu file. Some PDF files are also made like that, mainly when they are the results of scanning paper books (the text layer is made by OCR).

2) Method 2: Image + Text

Probably the best method, but more sophisticated than the first one, is to add on each ePub page a bitmap image (JPEG, possibly PNG) which is made of all bitmap and vector images of the PDF page, or bitmap and vector images (wripped in a SVG file). The text is not converted in a bitmap image or inserted in the SVG file, but added on the ePub page by using XHTML and CSS. The CSS uses: a) absolute positioning to put the text at the exact same place than in the PDF page; b) styles and fonts for the text to look exactly the same as in the PDF page. These two last steps are challenging, because HTML/CSS cannot always do what the PDF format can; lots of free and commercial tools exist, but most of the time cannot do that correctly when it comes to fixed layout.

3) Method 3: SVG only

The bitmap images, the vector images, and the text are embedded in SVG files (one SVG per page). The text should be rendered as true text (with fonts), not just outlines of the glyphs (vector images). Also called: SVG in the spine (no XHTML).

About the SVG file format: Scalable Vector Graphics (SVG) is an XML-based format for two-dimensional graphics with support for interactivity and animation. The SVG specification is an open standard developed by the *World Wide Web Consortium* (W3C) since 1999. That format is mainly used for vector images (created with programs like *Adobe Illustrator* or *InkScape*), but is more than just a vector image file format. SVG is in fact a document file format, more like the PDF format is, which can content bitmap images, vector images, and texts with their fonts embedded.

In fact, we can divide the number of methods in six, from the simplest to most sophisticated:

Method 1.1: one XHTML file per page with:
• one JPG or PNG bitmap image including the bitmap images, the vector images, and the text.

Method 1.2: one XHTML file per page with:
• one JPG or PNG bitmap image including the bitmap images, the vector images, and the text;
• one layer of hidden text on top of the image (accessible text).

Method 2.1: one XHTML file per page with:
• one JPG or PNG bitmap image including the bitmap and vector images;
• one layer of visible text on top of the image (accessible text);
• the font files.

Method 2.2: one XHTML file per page with:
• one SVG file including the bitmap and vector images;
• one layer of visible text on top of the image (accessible text);
• the font files.

Method 2.3 ([1]): one XHTML file per page with:
• one SVG file including the bitmap images, the vector images, and the text and fonts.

Method 3.1: one SVG file per page including the bitmap images, the vector images, and the text and fonts.

In the following of this book, I will only focus on the second method (image + text).

([1]) This method does not really make sense as the ePub format permits the SVG to be directly referenced in the "spine". See method 3.1.

Conversion Tools

Hereafter some free, open source, and commercial PDF to fixed layout ePub conversion tools:

Magic ePub (www.magicepub.com)

• Online service based in Germany.
• Price: 0.9 EUR/page; free is with a watermark on all converted pages and with only some pages converted at random.
• Conversion methods: the three methods are available (using partly *PDFTron*)[1].
• Parameters:
– Output size (small/1.4Mpx, medium/1.7Mpx, large/1.9Mpx, larger/2.4Mpx, retina/3.1Mpx)
– Image format (JPEG, PNG8)
– Image quality (full/100%, high/90%, medium/80%, low/70%)
– Output format (ePub3-fxl, Apple KF8)

---

[1] The "SVG in the spine" method seems not to work. I did not got any SVG files when I tried it.

Boosez (pdf2epub.boosez.com)

• Online service based in India.
• Price: free.
• Conversion methods: method 2 only (using *pdf2htmEX*).
• Conversion parameters: none (image format: PNG24, font format: OTF-TTF).

PDFTron (www.pdftron.com)

• Online services, command line programs, software libraries, etc.
• Price for the online service: 29 USD/month for 100 documents/month & 5000 pages/month; free is with a watermark on all converted pages.
• Conversion methods: method 2 for PDF to ePub, but a lot of other conversions are available (PDF to HTML, PDF to SVG, etc.)

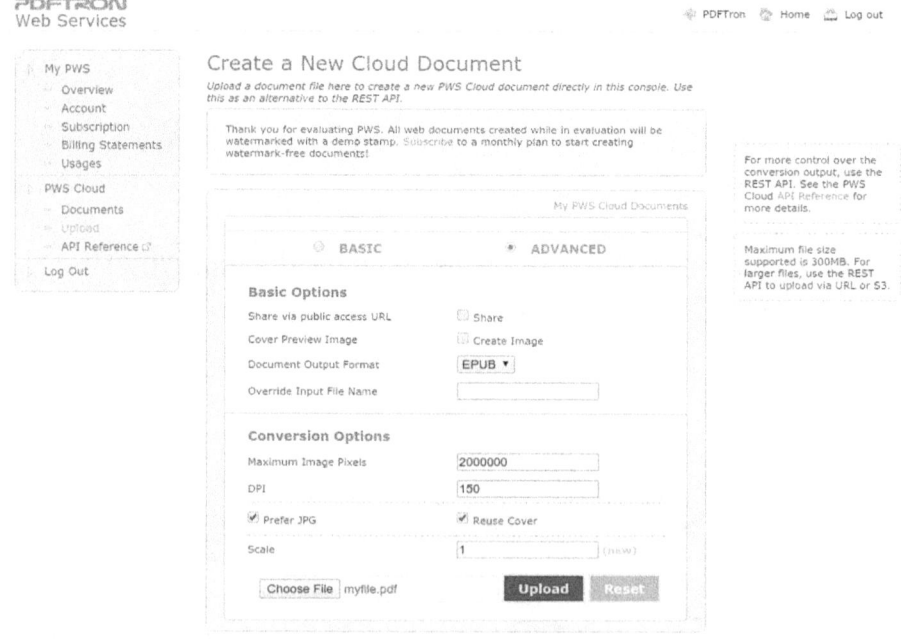

PDFTron PWS Web interface.

- *PDFTron PWS* (PDFTron Web Services): Online conversions. Maximum file size supported is 300 MB. For larger files, use the REST API to upload via URL or S3.
- *PDFTron Docpub*: Command line program available for *Windows*, *Linux*, and *Mac OS X*.

To install *Docpub* on *Linux*:

Download the trial file:

```
$ wget https://www.pdftron.com/downloads/docpub.tar.gz
```

Un-archive the downloaded file in the desired directory:

```
$ tar xzvf docpub.tar.gz
```

That's it. The executables are:

`docpub` (32 bit)
`docpub64` (64 bit)

Parameters:

`--format (-f) arg` → Output format (arg=epub in our case)
`--jpg_quality arg` → From 1 to 100
`--max_image_pixels arg` → In pixels; default: 2000000 pixels
`--dpi arg` → In dpi; default: 150 dpi
`--prefer_jpg arg` → true: jpeg, false: png; default: true

Basic conversion:

```
$ docpub -f epub myfile.pdf
```

Result: `myfile.epub` (with jpeg images and otf fonts).

Logo of pdf2htmlEX.

pdf2htmlEX (coolwanglu.github.io/pdf2htmlEX)

This tool, as its name tells us, does a conversion of the PDF pages to HTML pages, and does not produce an ePub file. To get an ePub3-fxl file, I will show how to use the result produced by *pdf2htmlEX* to create the ePub3-fxl file. It means mainly: a) remove the HTML viewer that *pdf2htmlEX* produces and integrates in the result; b) create all the files required by the ePub format and wrap the result into one unique file.

The tool and the method I will describe hereafter is free, and give a very good result for the visual aspect and for the text accessibility. This tool is developed by Lu Wang (pseudo: coolwanglu), a Chinese PhD student at the Department of Computer Science and Engineering of the Hong Kong University of Science and Technology.

PDF to HTML Conversion

The present version of *pdf2htmlEX* is 0.12 (released in July 2014). The tool supports JPEG and PNG background images (bitmap only), and since version 0.12, also SVG background images (bitmap and vector).

The original version of *pdf2htmlEX* is produced for the *Linux* operating system, but ported versions exist:

- For *Windows* (PC):

    soft.rubypdf.com/software/pdf2htmlex-windows-version
http://epubtest.org/results/
- For *OS X* (Mac):

    www.github.com/iapain/pdf2htmlex-macport

Install pdf2htmlEX

On Linux Debian/Ubuntu/Mint:

To install version 0.11 using the Lu Wang's package repository:

    www.launchpad.net/~coolwanglu/+archive/ubuntu/pdf2htmlex

```
$ sudo add-apt-repository ppa:coolwanglu/pdf2htmlex
$ sudo aptitude update
$ sudo aptitude install pdf2htmlex
```

To install or upgrade to the version 0.12 (but without SVG support), you can use the Debian's package repository:

packages.debian.org/sid/pdf2htmlex

Remark: As from now, no RPM package seems to exist for RedHat / CentOS / Fedora.

On Windows:

To install version 0.12 with SVG support:

soft.rubypdf.com/software/pdf2htmlex-windows-version
www.dropbox.com/s/ll8lsz9tjej6awo/pdf2htmlEX-0.12.7z

– Download the `pdf2htmlEX-0.12.7z` file.
– Unarchive the .7z file (with *WinZip* for example) in your home directory or somewhere else.
– Open the Command Prompt / DOS window and go to the directory you have chosen.
– That's it. The executable file to use is `pdf2htmlEX.exe`.

Poppler, *FontForge* and *Cairo* are external libraries needed by *pdf2htmlEX*.

Poppler is a free software utility library for rendering PDF documents. It is commonly used on GNU/Linux systems, and is used by the PDF viewers of the open source GNOME and KDE desktop environments.

FontForge is a full-featured font editor which supports all common font formats. FontForge is free software and is distributed under the 3-clause BSD license. It is available for several operating systems (including Linux, Windows and Mac OS X) and is localized into 12 languages. To facilitate automated format conversion and other repetitive tasks, Fontforge implements two scripting languages: its own language and Python. FontForge can run scripts from its GUI, from the command line, and also offers its features as a Python module so it can be integrated into any Python program.

Cairo is a library used to provide a vector graphics-based, device-independent API for software developers. It is designed to provide primitives for 2-dimensional drawing across a number of different backends. Cairo is designed to use hardware acceleration when available.

Make the conversion

By default, *pdf2htmlEX* produces one HTML file (`.html`) which includes every pages and everything needed to display them:

- page files (`.html`, `.page`)
- stylesheet files (`.css`)
- font files (`.woff`, `.otf`, `.ttf`, `.svg`)
- image files (`.jpg`, `.png`, `.svg`)
- javascript files (`.js`)
- a viewer (`.html`, `.css`, `.js`, `.png`, `.outline`)

The basic conversion is as follow:

```
$ pdf2htmlEX mybook.pdf
```

The result will be:

```
myfile.html
```

To produce the HTML files needed to make the ePub file, I use a lot of options for the conversion:

```
$ pdf2htmlEX --embed-css 0 --embed-font 0 --embed-image 0
   --embed-javascript 0 --embed-outline 0 --split-pages 1
   --bg-format jpg --hdpi 150 --vdpi 150 --fit-width 1275
   --fit-height 1650 --css-filename mybook.css
   --correct-text-visibility 1 mybook.pdf
```

The `--fit-width` and `--fit-height` parameters (in pixels) have to be adapted to fit your eBook. It will become the `viewport` parameter in the ePub file.

Example to compute the `viewport`:

– Paper book size (PDF): 8.5" × 11.0" ([1])
– Bitmap image resolution (PDF): 150 dpi ([2])

$$\text{Viewport (in pixels)} = [\text{resolution (dpi)} \times \text{width (inches)}] \times [\text{resolution (dpi)} \times \text{height (inches)}]$$

Viewport = (150 × 8.5) × (150 × 11.0) = 1275 px × 1650 px

Table for the 8.5" × 11" (letter) format:

```
150 dpi = 1275 px × 1650 px
144 dpi = 1224 px × 1584 px
100 dpi =  850 px × 1100 px
 96 dpi =  816 px × 1056 px
 72 dpi =  612 px ×  792 px
```

([1]) If in cm: 1 inch = 2.54 cm.
([2]) For eBooks, it should be 72, 96, 100, 144 or 150 dpi maximum; for printed books, it should be 300 dpi.

Parameters description:

0 = off, 1 = on

`--embed-css` 0 → Do not embed the CSS in the HTML file.
`--embed-font` 0 → Do not embed the fonts.
`--embed-image` 0 → Do not embed the images.
`--embed-javascript` 0 → Do not embed the javascripts.
`--embed-outline` 0 → Do not embed the outline.
`--split-pages` 1 → Split each PDF page into one HTML file.
`--bg-format` jpg → Save the bitmap images in JPEG format.
`--fit-width` 1275 → Original width of the pages (in pixels).
`--fit-height` 1650 → Original height of the pages (in pixels).
`--css-filename` mybook.css → Name of the CSS file.

By default, fonts will be WOFF (Web Open Font Format), but OTF, TTF, or SVG can be chosen also (use the `--font-format` parameter).

Let's assume `mybook.pdf` has 10 pages. The result will then be as follow (all files in the same directory as the PDF file):

Main file:

`mybook.html`

This is the file that you can view in the browser. The viewer code is not needed; a part of the code will need to be transferred into the `.page` files; after that, this file is no more needed.

Page files:

mybook1.page → Page 1 (the cover)
mybook2.page → Page 2
mybook3.page → Page 3
mybook4.page → Page 4
mybook5.page → Page 5
mybook6.page → Page 6
mybook7.page → Page 7
mybook8.page → Page 8
mybook9.page → Page 9
mybook10.page → Page 10

These files contain HTML code and will be renamed into .xhtml and then adapted with code coming from mybook.html. There is a .page file for each PDF page.

Image files:

bg = background

bg1.jpg → Image of the page 1
bg5.jpg → Image of the page 5
bg8.jpg → Image of the page 8
bg9.jpg → Image of the page 9
bga.jpg → Image of the page 10 (10 in decimal = A in hexadecimal)

There is a .jpg file only if there are bitmap and/or vector images on the PDF page. Be aware that a simple horizontal thin line is a vector image; that vector image will be converted into a bitmap image.

CSS files:

Will be needed for the ePub file:

`mybook.css` → CSS specific to mybook.
`base.min.css` → Generic CSS file; same for all conversion.

Will not be needed for the ePub file:

`fancy.min.css`
`pdf2htmlEX.min.js`
`compatibility.min.js`

Font files:

These files will be embedded in the ePub file. The number of font files depends of the number of fonts used in the document.

`f1.woff` → Font file n° 1
`f2.woff` → Font file n° 2
`f3.woff` → Font file n° 3
`f4.woff` → Font file n° 4
`f5.woff` → Font file n° 5
`f6.woff` → Font file n° 6
`f7.woff` → Font file n° 7
`f8.woff` → Font file n° 8

`mybook.outline`: Outline of mybook (will not be needed for the ePub file).

`pdf2htmlEX-64x64.png`: *pdf2htmlEX* logo (will not be needed for the ePub file).

Adapt the result

After removing all the unneeded files, and renaming the `.page` files into `.xhtml` files, this is the file list we have:

- **XHTML files:** `mybook1.xhtml, mybook2.xhtml, mybook3.xhtml, mybook4.xhtml, mybook5.xhtml, mybook6.xhtml, mybook7.xhtml, mybook8.xhtml, mybook9.xhtml, mybook10.xhtml.`

- **Image files:** `bg1.jpg, bg5.jpg, bg8.jpg, bg9.jpg, bga.jpg.`

- **CSS files:** `mybook.css, base.min.css.`

- **Font files:** `f1.woff, f2.woff, f3.woff, f4.woff, f5.woff, f6.woff, f7.woff, f8.woff.`

If you click on the XHTML files, there will be an error displayed in the browser. Some code from `mybook.html` has to be inserted in each XHTML files.

At the beginning of each XHTML files, add this portion of XML/HTML code coming from the `mybook.html` file:

```
<?xml version='1.0' encoding='UTF-8'?>
<html xmlns:epub="http://www.idpf.org/2007/ops"
   xmlns="http://www.w3.org/1999/xhtml">
 <head>
  <meta charset="utf-8"/>
  <meta name="generator" content="pdf2htmlEX"/>
  <link rel="stylesheet" type="text/css" href="base.min.css"/>
  <link rel="stylesheet" type="text/css" href="mybook.css"/>
  <meta name="viewport" content="width=1275, height=1650"/>
  <title></title>
 </head>
 <body>
  <div id="page-container">
```

At the end of each XHTML files, add this portion of HTML code:

```
  </div>
 </body>
</html>
```

In the `viewport` tag, the `width` and `height` parameters (in pixels) have to be adapted to fit your eBook (same as in the *pdf2htmlEX* command).

For *pdf2htmlEX* version 0.11 only: Some small adaptations have been made in the code taken from the `mybook.html` file. Because the files are XHTML, and not just HTML, the XML rules have to be followed, and the tags always need to have a corresponding end tags:

```
<TAG  .... >         → Not OK
<TAG  ...  />        → OK
<TAG> ...  </TAG>    → OK
```

Now, if you click on each XHTML files, the eBook pages should be displayed correctly in the browser window.

Using the SVG format in place of the JPG or PNG formats for the background images:

When using the SVG format for the background images, the vector images from a PDF page will be included in one SVG file also as vector images, and not converted in one bitmap image as it was the case previously. We can now have bitmap and vector images on the ePub pages. Even if this is an improvement, some ePub readers will not work properly if the SVG format is used.

To use the SVG format with *pdf2htmlEX*, the following parameter as to be:

```
--bg-format svg
```

Example of *pdf2htmlEX* conversion:

Input (PDF page): 3 bitmap images + 2 vector images

- With JPG background images (`--bg-format jpg`):

Output (ePub page): 1 JPG file including 1 bitmap image

– If there is no images on the PDF page, there will be no JPG file.
– The size (in pixels) of the JPG image will be the size of the smallest rectangle including the 5 images (smaller or equal to the viewport size).

- With SVG background images (`--bg-format svg`):

Output (ePub page): 1 SVG file including 3 bitmap images + 2 vector images

– Even if there is no images on the PDF page, there will be a SVG file (empty).
– The size (in pixels) of the SVG image is always equal to the viewport size.

pdf2htmlEX produces SVG file with the version equal to 1.2. This is not accepted by the ePub version 3 specifications. It will maybe not be a problem for the ePub reader, but it will not pass the ePub check validation process.

Unless there is really SVG 1.2 features used in the SVG files, you can safely just change the version parameter in the SVG file from 1.2 to 1.1. As the SVG files are just XML text files, it can be easily modified.

In *Linux*, you can use the following `sed` command to change all the SVG files present in the working directory:

```
$ sed -i -e s/version=\"1.2\"/version=\"1.1\"/g *.svg
```

In the `content.opf` file, in the `<manifest>` part, it is mandatory to add the `svg` property for XHTML items having SVG included in them. E.g.:

```
<item id="p1" href="p1.xhtml"
   media-type="application/xhtml+xml" properties="svg"/>
```

For now, the support for ePub3-fxl using XHTML with SVG background is as follow:

Not supported:

– Google Play Books (version 3.1.49) (but the "SVG in the spine" is supported)

Supported:

– Gitden (version 4.4.4)
– Readium (version 2.15.2)
– Adobe Digital Edition (version 4.0)

To see the ePub version 3 support of different eBook readers, you can go to:

www.epubtest.org/results/

HTML to ePub Conversion

All ePub files are in fact ZIP archives with the following file structure:

```
mimetype
META-INF/
OEBPS/
```

The `mimetype` file is the same for all ePub files. Its content is just:

```
application/epub+zip
```

The `META-INF` directory contains one or two files:

`container.xml`:

```
<?xml version='1.0' encoding='UTF-8'?>
<container xmlns="urn:oasis:names:tc:opendocument:xmlns:
   container" version="1.0">
 <rootfiles>
  <rootfile full-path="OEBPS/content.opf"
     media-type="application/oebps-package+xml"/>
 </rootfiles>
</container>
```

`com.apple.ibooks.display-options.xml` (only needed to be compatible with *Apple iBooks*):

```
<?xml version='1.0' encoding='UTF-8'?>
<display_options>
 <platform name="*">
  <option name="fixed-layout">true</option>
  <option name="specified-fonts">true</option>
 </platform>
</display_options>
```

For our purpose, these two files can be the same for all ePub files.

The `OEBPS` directory is where all the content is placed (this directory can have another name if correctly referenced in the `container.xml` file). All the files produced above will have to go into that directory, including three more files:

`content.opf`: References to all the files with their type (manifest) and page order (spine).
`nav.xhtml`: Table of content.
`cover.jpg`: Image of the eBook cover.

Create the content.opf file

The `content.opf` file should look like this:

```
<?xml version='1.0' encoding='UTF-8'?>
<package xmlns="http://www.idpf.org/2007/opf"
   prefix="rendition: http://www.idpf.org/vocab/rendition/#"
   unique-identifier="pub-id" version="3.0">
 <metadata xmlns:dc="http://purl.org/dc/elements/1.1/">
  <dc:identifier id="pub-id">123456789</dc:identifier>
  <dc:title>The Best Book in the World</dc:title>
  <dc:creator>John Doe</dc:creator>
  <dc:publisher>Big Bang Editions</dc:publisher>
  <dc:language>en</dc:language>
  <dc:description>This book is about ebooks.</dc:description>
  <meta content="cover_image" name="cover"/>
  <meta property="dcterms:modified">2014-05-22T12:00:00Z</meta>
  <meta property="rendition:layout">pre-paginated</meta>
  <meta property="rendition:orientation">auto</meta>
```

```xml
    <meta property="rendition:spread">auto</meta>
</metadata>
<manifest>
 <item id="page1" href="mybook1.xhtml" media-type="application/xhtml+xml"/>
 <item id="page2" href="mybook2.xhtml" media-type="application/xhtml+xml"/>
 <item id="page3" href="mybook3.xhtml" media-type="application/xhtml+xml"/>
 <item id="page4" href="mybook4.xhtml" media-type="application/xhtml+xml"/>
 <item id="page5" href="mybook5.xhtml" media-type="application/xhtml+xml"/>
 <item id="page6" href="mybook6.xhtml" media-type="application/xhtml+xml"/>
 <item id="page7" href="mybook7.xhtml" media-type="application/xhtml+xml"/>
 <item id="page8" href="mybook8.xhtml" media-type="application/xhtml+xml"/>
 <item id="page9" href="mybook9.xhtml" media-type="application/xhtml+xml"/>
 <item id="page10" href="mybook10.xhtml" media-type="application/xhtml+xml"/>
 <item id="image-page1" href="bg1.jpg" media-type="image/jpeg"/>
 <item id="image-page5" href="bg5.jpg" media-type="image/jpeg"/>
 <item id="image-page8" href="bg8.jpg" media-type="image/jpeg"/>
 <item id="image-page9" href="bg9.jpg" media-type="image/jpeg"/>
 <item id="image-page10" href="bga.jpg" media-type="image/jpeg"/>
 <item id="font1" href="f1.woff" media-type="application/font-woff"/>
 <item id="font2" href="f2.woff" media-type="application/font-woff"/>
 <item id="font3" href="f3.woff" media-type="application/font-woff"/>
 <item id="font4" href="f4.woff" media-type="application/font-woff"/>
 <item id="font5" href="f5.woff" media-type="application/font-woff"/>
 <item id="font6" href="f6.woff" media-type="application/font-woff"/>
 <item id="font7" href="f7.woff" media-type="application/font-woff"/>
 <item id="font8" href="f8.woff" media-type="application/font-woff"/>
 <item id="base-min-css" href="base.min.css" media-type="text/css"/>
 <item id="mybook-css" href="mybook.css" media-type="text/css"/>
 <item id="cover_image" href="cover.jpg" media-type="image/jpeg"
    properties="cover-image"/>
 <item id="nav" href="nav.xhtml" media-type="application/xhtml+xml"
    properties="nav"/>
</manifest>
<spine>
 <itemref idref="page1" properties="page-spread-right"/>
 <itemref idref="page2" properties="page-spread-left"/>
 <itemref idref="page3" properties="page-spread-right"/>
 <itemref idref="page4" properties="page-spread-left"/>
 <itemref idref="page5" properties="page-spread-right"/>
 <itemref idref="page6" properties="page-spread-left"/>
 <itemref idref="page7" properties="page-spread-right"/>
 <itemref idref="page8" properties="page-spread-left"/>
 <itemref idref="page9" properties="page-spread-right"/>
 <itemref idref="page10" properties="page-spread-left"/>
</spine>
<guide>
```

```
    <reference type="cover" title="Cover" href="p1.xhtml"/>
    <reference type="text" title="Text" href="p2.xhtml"/>
  </guide>
</package>
```

In the `package` tag, `version="3.0"` means ePub version 3.

For your own eBook, you have to adapt the `metadata`, the `item` and `itemref` fields.

There are three mandatory parts in the file:

• metadata:

This part includes:

a) The list of the bibliographic data of the book (DC = Dublin Core bibliographic references), like: an identifier (e.g. ISBN), the title, the author, the publisher, the publication date, etc.

b) The properties of the ePub. The following properties are specific to a fixed layout ePub:

```
<meta property="rendition:layout">pre-paginated</meta>
<meta property="rendition:orientation">auto</meta>
<meta property="rendition:spread">auto</meta>
```

Pre-paginated means fixed layout.

For a flowing text ePub, you will have:

```
<meta property="rendition:layout">reflowable</meta>
```

If the `rendition:layout` property is omitted in the ePub file, it will be considered reflowable by default.

• manifest:

This part lists all the files included in the ePub file with their type (`MIME-type`) and location (`href`). The location has to give the relative path to the file (e.g. `bg1.jpg` if the images are in the root directory; `images/bg1.jpg` if the images are in a subdirectory reserved for the images).

• spine:

This part gives the default page reading order.

The `guide` part is not mandatory.

Create the nav.xhtml file

The `nav.xhtml` file should look like this:

```
<?xml version='1.0' encoding='UTF-8'?>
<html xmlns:epub="http://www.idpf.org/2007/ops"
   xmlns="http://www.w3.org/1999/xhtml">
<head>
 <title>The Best Book in the World</title>
</head>
<body>
 <nav epub:type="toc" id="toc">
  <ol>
   <li>
    <a href="mybook3.xhtml">Title page</a>
   </li>
   <li>
    <a href="mybook4.xhtml">Copyright page</a>
   </li>
   <li>
    <a href="mybook5.xhtml">Chapter 1</a>
   </li>
   <li>
    <a href="mybook7.xhtml">Chapter 2</a>
```

```
   </li>
  </ol>
 </nav>
 <nav epub:type="landmarks">
  <ol>
   <li>
    <a epub:type="cover" href="mybook1.xhtml">Cover</a>
   </li>
   <li>
    <a epub:type="bodymatter" href="mybook2.xhtml">Bodymatter</a>
   </li>
  </ol>
 </nav>
 <nav epub:type="page-list" hidden="">
  <ol>
   <li>
    <a href="mybook1.xhtml">1</a>
   </li>
   <li>
    <a href="mybook2.xhtml">2</a>
   </li>
   <li>
    <a href="mybook3.xhtml">3</a>
   </li>
   <li>
    <a href="mybook4.xhtml">4</a>
   </li>
   <li>
    <a href="mybook5.xhtml">5</a>
   </li>
   <li>
    <a href="mybook6.xhtml">6</a>
   </li>
   <li>
    <a href="mybook7.xhtml">7</a>
   </li>
   <li>
    <a href="mybook8.xhtml">8</a>
   </li>
   <li>
    <a href="mybook9.xhtml">9</a>
   </li>
   <li>
    <a href="mybook10.xhtml">10</a>
   </li>
  </ol>
```

```
</nav>
</body>
</html>
```

Adapt the base.min.css file

In the `base.min.css` file, remove two times the following code:

```
;unicode-bidi:bidi-override
```

This is because the official ePub version 3 specifications indicate that "the `direction` and `unicode-bidi` properties must not be included in an EPUB Stylesheet. Authors should use appropriate HTML5 markup to express directionality information instead." If you do not remove it, an error will appear during the ePub file validation step (epubcheck).

Zip the content

To make the final ePub file, you have to zip all the files and directories into a ZIP file, and to rename the `.zip` extension into a `.epub` extension.

Please note that the `mimetype` file:

• should be the first file in the ZIP archive;
• should not be compressed.

Do the following from the root of the content directory (where the `mimetype` file and the two directories are located):

1) Create the `mybook.zip` archive with only one file in it (`mimetype`) and without using compression (-0):

```
$ zip -X -0 mybook.zip mimetype
```

2) Add all the rest of the content (`-r *`) but without the `mimetype` file (`-x mimetype`):

```
$ zip -X mybook.zip -r * -x mimetype
```

3) Rename the `.zip` file extension into `.epub`:

```
$ mv mybook.zip mybook.epub
```

`-X` → do not save extra file attributes
`-r` → recursive (include directories)
`-x` → exclude

Validate the result

To be sure your ePub file respects all the ePub version 3 specifications and will be accepted in case you upload it to an online eBook store, you have to check it. The best is to use the *epubcheck* application.

If your file is smaller than 10 MB, you can use the IDPF online validator:

validator.idpf.org

You can also install *epubcheck* on your computer.

On *Linux*:

Install *epucheck*:

```
$ sudo aptitude install epubcheck
```

Check a file:

```
$ epubcheck mybook.epub
```

Output in case of no problems are found:

```
Epubcheck Version 3.0.1
Validating against EPUB version 3.0
No errors or warnings detected.
```

The check will last some seconds. If errors or warnings are displayed after the check, you will have to edit your ePub file to correct them.

An ePub file with errors or warnings will maybe display correctly in some readers, but if you want to upload it to an online store, they will check the file and refuse it if there are errors or warnings.

You can also download the *Pagina ePup Checker* (version 1.3.0 for now) which is a Java graphical interface using *epubcheck*. Download the application from here for *Windows*, *Mac*, or *Linux*:

www.pagina-online.de/produkte/epub-checker/

On *Linux*:

```
$ wget http://download.pagina-online.de/epubchecker/files/
   pagina-EPUB-Checker_Linux-1.3.0.tar.gz
$ tar xzvf pagina-EPUB-Checker_Linux-1.3.0.tar.gz
```

To launch the graphical application:

```
$ ./paginaEPUBChecker.jar
```

The application window will then open. Select the `.epub` file to check.

2.0 — v15

www.ingramcontent.com/pod-product-compliance
Lightning Source LLC
Chambersburg PA
CBHW051826170526
45167CB00005B/2180